He
1

Holy Ground

By

D. M. Larson

HOLY GROUND BY D. M. LARSON FROM FREEDRAMA.NET

"The whole course of human history may depend on a change of heart in one solitary and even humble individual - for it is in the solitary mind and soul of the individual that the battle between good and evil is waged and ultimately won or lost."
- M. Scott Peck

CAST OF CHARACTERS

ART: A leader who holds everyone together. Husband of Bea.

BEA: A spiritual person who helps guide the group. Wife of Art.

DELIA: A wise cracking loner who decides to seek safety in numbers.

JUDE: A priest who wishes to protect everyone.

MOLLY: An amazing singer who has a special gift that disturbs the evil.

TURK: Companion to Molly who has been touched by the evil and is battling to be free.

TIME AND PLACE
A church in the near future.

PROLOGUE - NO DELIVERANCE FROM THIS EVIL

In near darkness, Molly approaches Turk who is on the floor
in pain. Molly wants to help him but is afraid.

>   MOLLY
>   Turk, what's wrong?

>   TURK
>   Don't get any closer. I don't want
>   to hurt you.

>   MOLLY
>   Why would you hurt me?

>   TURK
>   I've been trying to hide them. I
>   wanted to protect you. I hid the
>   truth from you. I wanted to keep
>   you safe.

>   MOLLY
>   Safe? Safe from what?

>   TURK
>   Look in to my eyes. Can you see
>   them? Can you see them looking out
>   at you? Can you see the darkness in
>   me? I want them out of me. I want
>   to rip them out of my soul. But
>   they cling to me. Holding on so
>   tight... so tight that I can't
>   breathe.

Turk grabs her. She is scared but doesn't pull away.

>   TURK
>   Can you show me how to get rid of
>   them? Can you help me?

>   MOLLY
>   I want to help. What can I do?

Turk pushes her away.

>   TURK
>   You're getting too close. I don't
>   want them to hurt you.

Turk pleads with something invisible that Molly can't see.

(CONTINUED)

                         TURK (CONT.)
              Please don't hurt her too. Please
              leave her alone. You have me... you
              don't need her too.

Molly grabs Turk and shakes him.

                         MOLLY
              Who are you talking to? Turk,
              there's nothing there.

                         TURK
              See what you've done. You've made
              them angry. They are punishing me.
              They always punish me. They want to
              punish you too.

Turk turns to Molly with an angry look in his eye and moves
toward her with his fists clenched.

                         MOLLY
              Stop. You're scaring me. What are
              you doing?!

                         TURK
              I can't let you! No! But I have
              to... it's the only way to make the
              pain inside me go away.

Turk moves to attack her and Molly screams. Turk falls to
the floor before he can touch her and lays still a moment.

                         MOLLY
              What happened to you? What's going
              on?

                         TURK
              Lift me up... I feel like I am
              falling... I'm drowning inside. You
              feel so far away. I feel like
              nothing can reach me. I'm lost. I'm
              so weak. Please... I can't take
              this much longer. I can't do this
              anymore. How can I live with this
              pain inside me?

                         MOLLY
              Then let me help you. Let me share
              the pain. Open up to me. Let me
              inside and I will fight this with
              you.

Turk jumps up and looks for a way out of the room.

                         TURK
               There's no place we can hide. We'll
               never escape them. Run! Run before
               they find you! I am hell bound.
               They are burned in my soul. They
               are a part of me. But there is
               still hope for you.

                         MOLLY
               I'm not leaving you. I'm here to
               stay. I will stay by your side and
               we can stop this together. Let me
               give you strength. Let me give you
               hope.

                         TURK
               Hope... there's no hope anymore...
               I'm too far gone... buried...
               buried deep inside this tomb...
               lost and undone. My kingdom has
               come, his will was done... I am
               beyond heaven and earth... there is
               no deliverance from this evil.

Turk turns on her again. He is crying now. She tries to
touch him but he pushes her away and falls to his knees

                         TURK (CONT.)
               Why are you still here? Save
               yourself. Please... you can't.
               You're not strong enough. You can't
               stop them.

He hisses his last line quietly like he is possessed.

                         TURK (CONT.)
               You can never take them from me.

                         END OF PROLOGUE

SCENE 1

An empty church waits in the night. Moonlight comes through
the windows. Monsters... horrible creatures are
heard. There is screaming. A couple runs inside the church.
A man (Art) has a shotgun and pauses at the open door. A
woman (Bea) rushes inside.

                    BEA
          Get down... get behind the pews...

                    ART
          They're stopping at the fence.

                    BEA
          Thank God. Save your bullets.

                    ART
          There's someone else out there
          trying to get through.

Bea goes to the door and looks. She is scared.

                    BEA
          You have to help them.

Art runs out yelling. Shotgun blasts are heard.

                    ART (OC)
          Come on!

                    BEA
          In here! It's safe.

Another couple comes in. The man (Turk) is hurt. The woman
(Molly) struggles to get him inside. Bea helps.

                    MOLLY
          Don't touch his arm... something is
          wrong with his arm.

                    TURK
          I don't know what they did to me.

                    MOLLY
          Does it still hurt?

                    TURK
          Don't worry... I will be okay.

                    BEA
          Can we put something on it?

                                        (CONTINUED)

                         MOLLY
          Maybe...

Art comes from the door scoops out some water from a holy
water receptacle. He goes up to Turk and pours it on his
arm. The arms steams in response. Molly and Bea
gasp. Turk yells and collapses. Molly cradles him.

                         BEA
          What did you do?

                         ART
          Those things out there are pure
          evil. I had a feeling the holy
          water might help.

                         MOLLY
          Help! I think he passed out from
          the pain.

                         TURK
          Shhh... it's okay...

                         MOLLY
          Turk?

                         TURK
          It helped. The holy water
          helped. I need to rest now. I can
          rest now.

Bea gets some robes from a side room and brings them. They
take Turk to a pew and lay him down. Bea takes something to
Art who is still guarding the door and then goes over to
Molly and offers her some food.

                         BEA
          Are you hungry?

                         MOLLY
          You sure you have enough? I don't
          want to take from you.

                         BEA
          We are in this together.

                         MOLLY
          In what? What is this?

                         BEA
          Evil. Evil walking among us.

                                              (CONTINUED)

                         MOLLY
          Why? What happened?

                         BEA
          There was too much going wrong...
          too many people walking the wrong
          road. They released something they
          couldn't control and it consumed
          them.

                         MOLLY
          There are so many.

                         BEA
          It's spreading... the sin. So much
          sin in the world.

                         MOLLY
          I didn't think I was that good.

                         BEA
          You must not be that bad either.

                         MOLLY
          How do we stop this? Can we stop
          it?

                         BEA
          I don't know... we have to stay
          strong... keep our faith
          strong. This church is our only
          protection. God is our only
          protection.

                         MOLLY
          I've always believed... but made a
          lot of mistakes.

                         BEA
          But you believe... and never wanted
          to be evil.

                         MOLLY
          Never.

Turk cries out. Molly goes to him.

                         MOLLY (CONT.)
          Turk? What's wrong?

Turk gets up and grabs his arm.

(CONTINUED)

                         TURK
                    It's coming back... it hurts so
                    bad.

Art comes over. He tries looking at Turk's arm.

                         TURK (CONT.)
                    It's fine.

Turk goes off to the side. Art goes up to Bea and pulls her
aside. Molly goes to Turk and checks on him.

                         ART
                    It doesn't look good. Even the
                    holy water isn't working.

                         BEA
                    Do you think it will spread?

                         ART
                    It might.

                         BEA
                    What will we do?

                         ART
                    We have to protect ourselves. Keep
                    them away from him. I'll stay
                    close to him. Those creatures
                    outside don't seem to be able to
                    get past the fence.

                         BEA
                    I'll see if I can keep Molly away
                    from him too.

                         ART
                    Please be careful. I don't want
                    you getting in his way. If he does
                    something, don't let it be you that
                    gets hurt... we have to be safe.

                         BEA
                    There's so few of us left. I want
                    to help them.

                         ART
                    I do too but I don't know what else
                    we can do for him.

                         BEA
                    I'll pray...

Bea moves away from Turk. Turk pulls away from Molly. Art
keeps an eye on them.

                    TURK
          Stop, Molly. I'll be okay.

                    MOLLY
          You're hurting again? It looks
          like it is coming back.

                    TURK
          No, it's fine.

                    MOLLY
          You're not fine. We have try
          something else.

                    TURK
          My head... what is with my head?

                    MOLLY
          What do you mean? What's going on?

                    TURK
          I'm seeing things...

                    MOLLY
          What kind of things?

                    TURK
          Horrible things?

                    MOLLY
          Try to think of something good...

                    TURK
          I can't.

Molly grabs a Bible.

                    MOLLY
          Here... read this...

                    TURK
          No!

He knocks it from her hand and holds his hand as if it is
hurt and moves away. Molly reaches for it and is
shaking. She is scared. Art goes to her and whispers.

                    ART
          Be careful.

                    MOLLY
          I don't understanding.

                    ART
          He's fighting... he's trying to
          fight the evil.

                    MOLLY
          He's a good man... he is...

                    ART
          There were a lot of good men...
          sometimes the evil is stronger.

                    MOLLY
          I can't lose him.

                    ART
          We don't want to lose him...

                    MOLLY
          We can't lose him.

Molly starts to go to him.

                    ART
          I don't know if that's wise right
          now. Let him calm down. Don't
          push too hard... or he might push
          back even harder.

Molly moves to a pew and puts down the Bible and
thinks. Art backs away but keeps an eye on Turk. Bea tries
to guide Molly away from Turk.

                    BEA
          Come sit with me over here.

                    MOLLY
          I have to do something... I can't
          stand by and let this happen to
          him... It was so horrible what
          happened to the others... I can't
          watch that happen to him too. I
          have to fight back.

Molly picks up a song book. She slowly flips through the
pages and finds a song. She walks down stage and the shadow
of a cross falls on her. She starts singing softly at
first... and then stronger. (Holy Holy Holy by Reginald
Heber). Bea goes up and join her.

                         SONG
          "Holy, holy, holy! Lord God
          Almighty / Early in the morning our
          song shall rise to Thee; / Holy,
          holy, holy, merciful and mighty /
          God in three Persons, blessed
          Trinity... etc."

Turk sits and turns away. Suddenly he cries out...

                         TURK
          Shut up!

Everyone stops.

                         TURK (CONT.)
          Stop that noise!

Bea moves away and Art moves in to guard them. Molly shakes
and slowly goes to Turk.

                         MOLLY
          What's wrong, Turk?

                         TURK
          The words... they burn me.

His arm is bad again... even worse than before.

                         MOLLY
          I'll stop. Please rest...

                         TURK
          How can I rest? The world is
          falling apart. Everything is being
          destroyed... we can't stop it... we
          can't do anything... we're lost.

Turk is angry and knocking things down and breaking
things. Art tries to get Molly away.

                         ART
          Please... back away...

                         MOLLY
          No... he'll be okay... please don't
          hurt him...

                         ART
          He's going to hurt you...

                          MOLLY
                No... he won't...

                          ART
                Listen to me...

Art grabs Molly who struggles. Bea helps. Turk charges.

                          TURK
                Leave my wife alone!

                          BEA
                Look out!

Turk is about to hit Art with something. Molly
screams. Bea jumps in the way and is hit by Turk and
falls. Art yells and lets go of Molly.

                          ART
                Bea! My love!

Molly cries out and picks up Art's shotgun and points it at
Turk.

                          MOLLY
                What did you do?

Turk drops his weapon.

                          TURK
                I'm sorry... I'm sorry...

Turk stumbles back in pain. He cries out... Molly raises
the shotgun. Turk growls and runs out the door. Molly
points the gun at the door still. Art gently lays her down.
Art goes to Molly and carefully takes the gun from her.

                          ART (CONT.)
                Sit.

Molly sits and Art goes to Bea.

                          MOLLY
                Will she be okay?

                          ART
                Yes.

Art tends to her wound. Molly is crying.

                          ART (CONT.)
                Be strong. Bea needs you to be
                strong.

                                              (CONTINUED)

                    MOLLY
          I'm so sorry... I'm so so sorry.

                    ART
          Please don't... please stay calm.

                    MOLLY
          What happened? What's happening?

Art goes to her and grabs her.

                    ART
          Don't do this... get it together.

Molly nods and calms down. Art goes back to Bea.

                    MOLLY
          How does she look?

                    ART
          She got hit here... in the head.
          It's not bleeding too much...
          that's good.

                    MOLLY
          Will she be okay?

                    ART
          Yes.

Then Delia appears at the door.

                    DELIA
          Hello?

Art jumps up and grabs the shotgun. Molly is at his side,
scared. Delia holds up her hands.

                    DELIA (CONT.)
          Hey! I'm a good guy.

Art relaxes and lowers gun.

                    ART
          How did you get past all the
          creatures? There must have been
          hundreds gathered there.

                    DELIA
          Not now... they're gone.

Art and Molly look at each other and go to the door to look.

                                        (CONTINUED)

                         MOLLY
               Where did they go?

                         DELIA
               They scattered... like they were
               afraid of something... I was
               watching from the roof of a
               building next door... the bank
               building... hard to break into...
               thought that would be safe... get
               it safe? ...little joke to lighten
               the mood.

                         ART
               What did you see?

                         DELIA
               Oh... um... I saw them suddenly
               move away from here as if something
               scared them. They seemed genuinely
               frightened... never seen those
               creatures scared of anything. I
               had to come see what was good
               enough to pull that off.

                         ART
               We have no idea. They won't enter
               the holy ground but I don't know
               what else we did.

                         MOLLY
               Turk wouldn't have anything to do
               with it would he?

                         ART
               Or the singing... you saw how the
               singing affected Turk...

                         DELIA
               Well, whatever it was... figure it
               out... we need more of it.

                         ART
               Are there many people in town
               left?

                         DELIA
               I haven't seen too many people
               around... little groups moving
               through... looking for food...

                         ART
               Do you have more food?

                         DELIA
               I've hoarded some... I shouldn't
               have left it behind.

Art looks outside.

                         ART
               There's no creatures now. You
               could go back for it.

                         DELIA
               Maybe.

                         MOLLY
               Don't go out there again... it's
               not safe.

                         ART
               We need food.

                         MOLLY
               We need to survive.

                         DELIA
               Look. I don't mind going
               back. Those creatures scattered
               pretty far. I don't think they'll
               be back soon, plus it's morning now
               and they don't care much for the
               sun.

                         MOLLY
               You don't mind coming back here?

                         DELIA
               This might be safer than where I
               was. I don't like being alone
               either. And if worse comes to
               worst... I would feel better being
               in a church in the end.

                         MOLLY
               I hope this won't be the end.

                         ART
               It won't.

                         DELIA
               Being around optimists would be
               nice too. Hard to be optimistic
               when you're alone.

                    ART
          You're okay getting the food alone
          though?

                    MOLLY
          I'll go with her.

                    ART
          You sure?

                    MOLLY
          I want a look outside.

                    ART
          I don't think you'll see him.

Molly ignores Art and looks at Delia.

                    MOLLY
          Should we go then?

                    DELIA
          Sure... the sooner we go, the
          better our chances to get back
          before dark.

                    ART
          Be careful.

Molly and Delia head for the door and open it. A man (Jude)
is standing there and they scream. Art rushes toward them
with his shotgun but Jude clearly isn't a danger. In fact,
he has a priest collared shirt on.

                    JUDE
          Sorry to alarm everyone.

                    ART
          It's all right, Father. We're all
          a bit jumpy.

                    JUDE
          Understandable. Where are you
          ladies going?

                    DELIA
          To get food. I have some stashed
          away.

                    JUDE
          Very wise... A good time since
          those creatures seem to have
          scattered.

                              MOLLY
                    Can we get a quick blessing Father?

Jude quickly blesses them with the sign of the cross.

                              JUDE
                    In the name of the Father, the Son
                    and the Holy Spirit, Amen. Go in
                    peace.

Molly and Delia do the sign of the cross with him. Jude
takes holy water and makes the sign of the cross on their
foreheads. Then they go. Art is back with his wife
checking on her. Jude joins them.

                              JUDE (CONT.)
                    How is she?

                              ART
                    She's been resting. She got hit
                    pretty hard... she needs time to
                    heal.

                              JUDE
                    I will pray over her.

                              ART
                    I need to talk to you first.

Art looks at Jude suspiciously.

                              ART (CONT.)
                    Where did you come from? What were
                    you doing out there?

                              JUDE
                    I was in the church storm
                    cellar. The entrance is
                    outside. I heard you all walking
                    around up here and could make out
                    some of what you were
                    saying. Then I heard the song and
                    could see the creatures
                    scattering...

                              ART
                    So you think it was the song that
                    did it?

                              JUDE
                    Most definitely.

                    ART
          Did you see the man run out of
          here?

                    JUDE
          No, not really.

                    ART
          I was wondering if there was a
          connection with him too.

                    JUDE
          Why do you suspect that?

                    ART
          Just a feeling... something about
          him was different than the
          others. He fought it longer.

                    JUDE
          Perhaps there was still a lot of
          good in him.

                    ART
          No doubt... I hadn't seen someone
          fight it so well before.

                    JUDE
          There are some of us that never
          followed the path of evil... we
          were saved the fate of the
          others. Evil was a choice, not an
          accident. He may represent some
          middle ground.

                    ART
          Maybe he walked the path of evil
          and then chose good again.

                    JUDE
          Perhaps... not something that
          happens often. Once they go down
          that road, most never return.

                    ART
          Molly, his wife, seems to have
          something powerful in her. Maybe
          it was powerful enough to bring him
          back.

                    JUDE
          That would be a blessing for us if
          that is true. We need something
          powerful on our side.

(CONTINUED)

Delia runs in with some supplies. She is upset.

                    ART
          What's wrong?

                    DELIA
          It's Molly... she ran off...

                    ART
          What? Why?

                    DELIA
          She saw someone at the end of the
          street watching us as we started to
          bring out supplies. She went to
          him.

                    ART
          Just now?

                    DELIA
          Yes.

                    ART
          I have to stop her.

                    JUDE
          Stay with your wife. I will go.

                    DELIA
          Down the street to the right... we
          saw someone on the corner of
          Lincoln and 2nd St.

Jude pulls out a holy water sprinkler and runs outside.

                    DELIA (CONT.)
          I'm so sorry I couldn't stop
          her. There's more supplies out
          there too... I couldn't carry them
          all by myself... I'll go back and
          get the rest.

                    ART
          Be careful... if there's one, there
          could be more.

                    DELIA
          Was that her husband she saw?

                    ART
          Probably... did she call out his
          name?

                    DELIA
          Something weird... Dirk?

                    ART
          Turk.

                    DELIA
          Yeah... that was it.

                    ART
          I wonder if it was him.

                    DELIA
          It was far away... I have no clue
          how she could see him.

                    ART
          She seems a little more aware than
          the rest of us.

                    DELIA
          She is different... distant but not
          in a bad way.

                    ART
          Like she's a little bit somewhere
          else.

                    DELIA
          Exactly... I better get the rest of
          the stuff in case anyone else is
          coming back for a visit.

                    ART
          This should be enough for
          now. Let's wait to get more until
          we're sure everything is safe.

                    DELIA
          Okay.

                    ART
          Thank you so much for sharing all
          this with us. This would have
          lasted a lot longer if you had
          stayed by yourself so I know this
          is a sacrifice.

                    DELIA
          Being alone was worse.

                          ART
               How long were you alone over there?

                          DELIA
               I don't know... a few weeks...
               there were some others there with
               me but they wanted to leave. They
               were hoping this was something just
               happening here. They voted to
               leave but I was too scared. I
               wouldn't go out there with all the
               creatures around.

                          ART
               How did you end up with so many
               supplies?

                          DELIA
               One of them took pity on me and
               left it... she really didn't think
               they had much of a chance but
               wanted to be with her husband...
               she figured they wouldn't need it
               as much... either they'd make it to
               a place without creatures and have
               plenty of food there or wouldn't
               make it anywhere and wouldn't need
               it either.

                          ART
               Logical.

                          DELIA
               To the end.

                          ART
               Did they make it?

                          DELIA
               I don't think so. I watched from
               the roof... they were swarmed. I
               can't see how they got away from
               that. They made it around the
               corner so I don't know what
               happened. I never got brave enough
               to go look.

                          ART
               Smart will keep you alive a lot
               longer than brave.

Jude returns with Molly.

                    DELIA
Why did you run off like that?

                    MOLLY
I'm so sorry... but I saw him... I
saw Turk.

                    ART
You were able to recognize him?

                    MOLLY
Yes, he didn't look like one of the
creatures... still mostly
himself. But when I moved toward
him he would move away. And when I
called out to him, he wouldn't
answer. I got scared when I
realized he led me pretty far from
here so I stopped and came back...
but then he followed me... keeping
the same distance. If I tried
going to him again, he would stop
and move away.

                    ART
So is he out there now?

                    MOLLY
Maybe.

                    ART
Why hasn't he changed... why isn't
he like the others who have been
infected?

                    MOLLY
Do you think there might be a way
to stop this infection from
spreading? Something about Turk
that's different?

                    ART
You'd know better than I would. Is
there anything Turk might have done
differently than the
rest? Anything about him that's
unique?

                    JUDE
He could be the key to a cure.

                                    MOLLY
                    I don't know... I can't think of
                    anything...

                                    ART
                    Keep thinking about it... something
                    might come to mind.

Bea wakes up and screams.

                                    BEA
                    They're coming! They're coming
                    back!

Art runs to her and holds her.

                                    ART
                    No, Bea... they're gone now...
                    you're safe.

                                    BEA
                    I saw them in my sleep... I see
                    them coming again... they want
                    something.

Jude is at the door watching now. Art looks to him and Jude
shakes his head.

                                    JUDE
                    Nothing outside.

                                    DELIA
                    Not yet anyway.

                                    BEA
                    I saw such horrible things in my
                    sleep... as if I was with them...
                    watching them... the ceremonies...
                    the sacrifice...

                                    DELIA
                    Has she had visions before?

                                    ART
                    Never.

                                    BEA
                    They are outside of town... hiding
                    in the woods... waiting... waiting
                    for darkness.

                         DELIA
          That sounds about right.

                         ART
          You were just having a nightmare,
          Bea. You're safe now.

Bea touches Art lovingly on the face.

                         BEA
          Where's Molly?

Molly goes to her.

                         MOLLY
          I'm here.

                         BEA
          Sing...

                         MOLLY
          What?

                         BEA
          Sing to me.

Art nods and gets a hymnal for Molly. Molly opens it and
searches for a song. When she gets to a certain page, Bea
says without looking:

                         BEA (CONT.)
          That one.

Molly looks at Art surprised but Art nods for her to sing.
Jude joins her at the chorus. Then there is horrible scream
outside and they freeze.

                         BEA
          Prepare yourselves... they're
          coming.

The lights fade to black.

                         END OF SCENE

SCENE 2 - CONFESSION

This scene is a flashback to a time before the
creatures. Lights are dim and focus on a corner of the
church which the confessional. We see Jude and Delia but
they are divided by a partition.

                    DELIA
          I'm scared, Father.

                    JUDE
          Scared? Of what?

                    DELIA
          Everything.

                    JUDE
          God will protect you.

                    DELIA
          I wish I could believe that.

                    JUDE
          You can trust God.

                    DELIA
          I fear God. I don't trust him. I
          am afraid what he is going to
          do. I am afraid of what will
          happen every day... If I go
          outside, what will be waiting for
          me? There's something wrong out
          there. Something's not right.

                    JUDE
          Things are changing. I have sensed
          it too.

                    DELIA
          What do we do?

                    JUDE
          Trust in God.

                    DELIA
          Back to that again... How can I
          trust him? How can I trust the
          one who took my father away? How
          can I trust the one who turned my
          mother into a drunk? How I trust
          the one who put me in the house of
          someone who abused me? Every day I
          lived in fear. What would happen
                    (MORE)

                                        (CONTINUED)

                        DELIA (cont'd)
          if I stepped outside my room?   I
          didn't know what was waiting for
          me. I never knew what would wake
          up that day. The creep, the angry
          one, the monster... I didn't even
          want to get out of bed anymore. It
          got too hard. I was too scared. I
          would hide and pray to God to help
          me. But God never did. My
          childhood gone and my only escape
          was adulthood.

                        JUDE
          You blamed God for all that?

                        DELIA
          Even if God didn't do it why did he
          let it happen?

                        JUDE
          He will never give you more than
          you can handle.

                        DELIA
          I can't handle it though... I'm
          going crazy.. The fear is crippling
          me... I have to drag myself out of
          bed and force myself to live each
          day... Sure, I put on this happy
          face... People think I am pretty
          cheerful... No one cares to see the
          pain under my skin... The pain
          that's ripping at my soul.

                        JUDE
          God sees.

                        DELIA
          I know.

                        JUDE
          Have you sinned?

                        DELIA
          What?

                        JUDE
          Are you a sinner?

                        DELIA
          I don't know...

                         JUDE
          Do you think about sinning?

                         DELIA
          All the time.

                         JUDE
          What stops you?

                         DELIA
          Fear... Fear of what might happen
          to me... See, I'm afraid of
          everything.

                         JUDE
          Your fear could be a blessing.

                         DELIA
          What?

                         JUDE
          It keeps you from doing wrong... It
          keep you from doing anything evil.

                         DELIA
          I hope so.

                         JUDE
          Do you feel tempted?

                         DELIA
          All the time.

                         JUDE
          What tempts you?

                         DELIA
          I'm tempted to give up... It's too
          hard to keep living.

                         JUDE
          Perhaps you need something to live
          for.

                         DELIA
          I do.

                         JUDE
          We will ask God to give you
          something to live for... We are all
          born with a purpose.

                    DELIA
          I just wish I knew what it is.

                 END OF SCENE

SCENE 3

In darkness, the creatures are heard. It sounds like even
more than before. Lights come up on everyone waiting
nervously, unsure what to do. Art is at the door with his
gun. Molly goes to look now and Delia joins her.

                    DELIA
          We can keep watch for a bit if you
          want to rest or get some food.

                    ART
          Thanks.

Art goes to check on Bea. Bea is asleep. Jude joins them.

                    JUDE
          How is she doing?

                    ART
          She is resting again.

                    JUDE
          Would you like me to say a prayer
          for her?

                    ART
          Please.

Bea wakes up suddenly.

                    BEA
          Not yet.

Suddenly the creatures stop making noise. Delia looks out
the door.

                    DELIA
          Oh my God! One of them came
          through the gate!

Art jumps in to action with his gun. Molly turns and waves
her arms.

                    MOLLY
          No, stop, wait!

                    ART
          Move!

                    MOLLY
          It's Turk!

(CONTINUED)

                         ART
          I said move.

                         MOLLY
          Please... don't...

                         ART
          He's one of them.

                         MOLLY
          Maybe... maybe not... maybe they
          don't fully have him yet... maybe
          he's finding a way to fight the
          evil... maybe he wants our help.

                         ART
          Maybe he's found a way to adapt...
          maybe he's the next step in their
          evolution... a missing link we
          can't allow to live.

Jude has moved to them. He carefully grabs Art's arm.

                         JUDE
          Peace brother.

                         ART
          Peace? Peace is when those
          creatures are back in Hell where
          they belong.

                         MOLLY
          Turk isn't evil...

                         ART
          Evil enough.

                         JUDE
          Please... let's see what is going
          on... but be ready.

                         ART
          I plan on it.

                         DELIA
          It's just the one still.

They all back away from the door. After a few moments Turk
comes through the door but he looks only a little human and
the rest of him is black and oozing.

                                        (CONTINUED)

                         MOLLY
               Turk?

                         TURK
               Come with me.

Turks voice is raspy, almost like a loud whisper.

                         MOLLY
               Where?

                         TURK
               Come... we need to leave here.

                         MOLLY
               And go where, Turk? Where will we
               go?

                         TURK
               Now.

Turk moves toward Molly and she backs away. Art steps in.

                         ART
               Back off.

                         TURK
               She's mine.

                         ART
               Not anymore.

Turk yells and lunges at Art. Bea jumps up.

                         BEA
               No!

Turk freezes and moves back a bit startled. Jude is close
now and sprinkles holy water on him. Turk screams and
knocks Jude to the ground. Delia goes to Jude and pulls him
away.

                         BEA (CONT.)
               Speak creature! Speak the truth!

Turk's voice is forceful.

                         TURK
               I've come to speak for the evil.

Turk's voice returns to the whisper.

                         TURK (CONT.)
               I've come to warn you. You are not
               safe here anymore.

Turk's voice is forceful again.

                         TURK (CONT.)
               We grow stronger and you are weak.

                         DELIA
               It's like he's talking in two
               voices.

                         MOLLY
               He's struggling. He's fighting it.

                         ART
               How? No one has before.

Bea moves a little closer.

                         BEA
               What do you want?

Turk's voice is a whisper.

                         TURK
               Molly.

Turk's voice is forceful.

                         TURK (CONT.)
               Molly!

                         MOLLY
               Why Turk? Why me?

Turk's voice is a whisper.

                         TURK
               I need your help.

Turk's voice is forceful.

                         TURK (CONT.)
               I need your strength.

                         MOLLY
               I can't go out there. They'd hurt
               me.

                    TURK
                (Whisper)
          Please.

                    TURK (CONT.)
                (Forceful)
          You must.

                    BEA
          Tell us why!

                    TURK
                (Forceful)
          She is the one. She is the
          reason. She is the beginning and
          the end. Alpha and Omega. Yin and
          Yang. She will bring balance.

Turk has moved closer to Molly and she is almost in a trance
and doesn't move. Art steps in with his gun pointed at
Turk.

                    ART
          Back off.

Turk grabs the gun and sticks it at his head.

                    TURK
                (Whisper)
          Do it. Do it. Do it. Now. Please.

Molly pulls Art back.

                    MOLLY
          No, Art. Please... no.

                    BEA
          Go!

Turk growls and heads for the door. He turns one more time
and looks at Molly.

                    BEA (CONT.)
          In the name of the Lord our God,
          leave this place!

Turk is gone. Bea starts to fall and Art helps her
down. She is out of it again. Delia struggles to get Jude
to the front.

                    ART
          What is going on?

(CONTINUED)

                         MOLLY
               Turk was struggling... he was
               fighting it.

                         ART
               And you're the key.

                         DELIA
               I need some help here.

Art and Molly go up to Delia and Jude.

                         ART
               How bad is he hurt?

                         DELIA
               No clue.

                         MOLLY
               I'll check him.

Molly examines Jude and Art goes to Bea.

                         ART
               Bea... Bea? It's like someone else
               is speaking through her.

Jude tries to sit up.

                         JUDE
               He didn't hit me that hard.

                         MOLLY
               Looks like he did to me.

                         JUDE
               I played football for Norte Dame...
               I can take a few hits.

Jude starts to get up and then stumbles.

                         MOLLY
               I think that was a few years ago.

                         JUDE
               A bit more than a few. I'll sit.

                         MOLLY
               I wish I knew what that was all
               about... What does this all have
               to do with me? I never was
               important before. I never was
               special. I'm not the most religious
                         (MORE)

                                              (CONTINUED)

                         MOLLY (cont'd)
          person. I was in the church choir
          because I loved to sing. I didn't
          really do much else. I've lived a
          good enough life but nothing
          unique... nothing miraculous. I
          don't know what to do. I have no
          direction. How can I do something
          important when I don't even feel
          important. I didn't chose this
          mission... I didn't ask God to make
          me a vessel or some tool. I didn't
          chose this, God. I didn't ask for
          this.

                         JUDE
          You may not have chosen God but God
          chose you.

                         MOLLY
          I'm not strong enough. I'll fail.

                         JUDE
          You can't...

                         MOLLY
          That's too much pressure. I've
          never been good under pressure.

                         DELIA
          Then get good fast because they're
          getting louder out there.

                         ART
          What's going on?

Delia grabs Art's gun.

                         DELIA
          I'll be happy to find out.

Delia goes outside and yells.

                         DELIA (CONT.)
          What's up, devil's spawn?

She fires a bunch of shots at them. Art runs to the door.

                         ART
          Get back in here. That's a waste
          of bullets.

Delia reenters.

                        DELIA
          Oh but it felt so good.

                        ART
          We've got to put our heads together
          and figure out what is going on.

                        DELIA
          Molly and your wife seem to be the
          key players here.

                        ART
          I don't know what's going on with
          Bea. She's never done anything
          like this before.

                        DELIA
          All of us our doing things
          different now... except for the
          priest... he's always been battling
          evil.

                        ART
          We all have in our own
          ways. That's why we're all still
          free.

                        DELIA
          Free? Sort of... not really.

                        ART
          We've spent so much time hiding in
          churches and gathering supplies...
          this is the first time something
          different has happened. This is
          new. We've never found so many
          others like us... and never had so
          many of them after us.

                        MOLLY
          They've been like that for me.

                        ART
          Always following you?

                        MOLLY
          Always.

                        ART
          And Turk?

                    MOLLY
          He protected me... but he knew
          something was different...
          something was very wrong. We tried
          to keep away from others... we
          didn't want anyone else to get
          hurt. But he was injured... and I
          had to find help.

                    ART
          It's okay, Molly. We're here for
          you. We're not going to send you
          away.

                    DELIA
          So you are what they are after.

                    MOLLY
          I'm so sorry... I don't know why
          though. I can't figure out what
          they want.

                    DELIA
          So if we just give them what they
          want...

                    ART
          Stop it! We won't talk that
          way. It's not going to happen that
          way... we can't let them win...
          this is the reason we're here...
          this is the reason we're fighting
          and resisting... we have a purpose.

                    MOLLY
          Delia's right... hand me over and
          save yourselves.

The creatures outside get louder and more excited.

                    JUDE
          But it won't happen that way... you
          think they'll stop once they get
          her? In fact, maybe they'll be
          unstoppable once they do have her.

                    MOLLY
          I will go to them. I won't
          endanger you anymore.

The creatures are in a frenzy.

                         DELIA
          Look, Molly. Maybe Jude's right...
          maybe giving them what they want is
          the worst thing we can do.

                         MOLLY
          I have to try something.

Molly goes to the door and opens it and suddenly there is
silence. Bea jumps up and goes to Jude.

                         BEA
          Now... now is the time for prayer.

                         JUDE
          Our father who art in heaven,
          hallowed be thy name...

Outside Turk yells.

                         TURK (OS)
          Come! Come to us!

Instead of going, Molly sings "How Great Thou Art"

                         MOLLY
          "O Lord my God, When I in awesome
          wonder, Consider all the worlds Thy
          Hands have made; I see the stars, I
          hear the rolling thunder, Thy power
          throughout the universe displayed."

Others join in:

                         OTHERS
          Then sings my soul, My Saviour God,
          to Thee, How great Thou art, How
          great Thou art. Then sings my soul,
          My Saviour God, to Thee, How great
          Thou art, How great Thou art!"

Turk calls out.

                         TURK (OS)
          Molly, please stop... you're
          hurting me!

Molly stops as do the others.

                         MOLLY
          Turk! Please come to me... I will
          help you.

                              TURK (OS)
                    It hurts... it all hurts so bad.

                              MOLLY
                    I will find a way to help you. I
                    will find a way to heal you.

                              TURK (OS)
                    I want to be free.

                              MOLLY
                    Then let me free you.

The creatures outside grow louder and angry. Turk appears
at the door. Molly reaches out and takes his hand. He
struggles to see in the light and looks in pain. She leads
him in to the church and to the altar. She gets Turk to
kneel and she kneels beside him.

                              MOLLY (CONT.)
                    Now pray, Turk. Ask God for help.

Bea goes to them and rests her hand on Turk.

                              BEA
                    We're all here for you. We all are
                    praying for you.

The others moves to the altar and lay their hands on each
other and bow their heads in prayer.

                              BEA (CONT.
                    Our Father in heaven, hallowed be
                    your name.

Other join in. Lights fade to black.

                              OTHERS
                    Your kingdom come, your will be
                    done, on earth as it is in heaven.
                    Give us this day our daily bread,
                    and forgive us our debts, as we
                    also have forgiven our debtors. And
                    lead us not into temptation...

In darkness:

                              BEA
                    ...but deliver us from evil.

                         END OF SCENE

SCENE 4 - WAYFARING STRANGER

This is a flashback. The lights are dim except for one spot
where Molly stands. Molly is in the church singing
"Wayfarin Stranger." Turk walks in unnoticed during the
song.

                    MOLLY
          "I'm just a poor wayfaring stranger
          I'm traveling through this world of
          woe
          Yet there's no sickness, toil nor
          danger
          In that bright land to which I go
          I'm going there to see my
          mother/father
          I'm going there no more to roam
          I'm only going over Jordan
          I'm only going over home

          I know dark clouds will gather
          'round me
          I know my way is rough and steep
          Yet golden fields lie just before
          me
          Where God's redeemed shall ever
          sleep
          I'm going there to see my
          father/mother
          S/he said he'd/she'd meet me when I
          come
          I'm only going over Jordan
          I'm only going over home

          I want to wear a crown of glory
          When I get home to that good land
          I want to shout salvation's story
          In concert with the blood-washed
          band
          I'm going there to meet my Saviour
          To sing his praise forever more
          I'm just a-going over Jordan
          I'm just a-going over home"

He listens and then claps when she is done. Molly is
startled.

                    MOLLY
          I didn't know anyone was here. I
          never sing in front of anyone.

(CONTINUED)

                         TURK
               Why? You're amazing.

                         MOLLY
               No... I'm not.

                         TURK
               I've never heard such an incredible
               voice. I listen and it does
               something to me. Something I've
               never felt before. It sends
               shivers down my spine. And then I
               feel this peace wash over me. I've
               never felt so peaceful. I felt
               drawn here by your song. I almost
               never set foot inside a church...
               but your song... your song brought
               me here... brought me to you.

                         MOLLY
               I know you, don't I?

                         TURK
               You do.

                         MOLLY
               You look so familiar.

                         TURK
               I was one of your
               students. Community service
               orientation. Don't worry. I
               wasn't one the ones required to be
               there. I volunteered.

                         MOLLY
               I remember now. We even did the
               roadside cleanup together.

                         TURK
               It's interesting what you find
               along a roadside.

                         MOLLY
               What was the most interesting thing
               you found that day?

                         TURK
               You.

Molly gets nervous.

(CONTINUED)

>   MOLLY
>   Stop.

Turk changes the subject a bit.

>   TURK
>   I remember we found a music box.

>   MOLLY
>   That's right.

>   TURK
>   I couldn't believe it still
>   worked. What was the song?

Molly sings.

>   MOLLY
>   "Oh, come, all ye faithful,
>   Joyful and triumphant!
>   Oh, come ye, oh, come ye to
>   Bethlehem;
>   Come and behold him
>   Born the king of angels:
>   Oh, come, let us adore him,
>   Oh, come, let us adore him,
>   Oh, come, let us adore him,
>   Christ the Lord."

>   TURK
>   That's right. I like your version
>   better.

>   MOLLY
>   I still have it.

>   TURK
>   Why did you keep it?

>   MOLLY
>   I keep lots of weird little
>   things. I know it was probably
>   important to someone. And
>   sometimes those things make me
>   happy and bring me new memories.

>   TURK
>   You have a beautiful way of looking
>   at things. Anyone ever told you
>   that?

                                        (CONTINUED)

                         MOLLY
No. Probably because I don't
usually share this much of myself
with anyone. It's like my
singing. I keep my feelings to
myself.

                         TURK
It's nice having someone to talk
to.

                         MOLLY
I know what you mean. Everyone in
this world seems so isolated.

                         TURK
You can have a million online
friends but never really talk to
anyone. Technology brought the
world closer together and but made
individuals grow farther apart.

                         MOLLY
You're a pretty smart guy.

                         TURK
I don't hear that very often.

                         MOLLY
I like how you think.

                         TURK
I like everything about you.

                         MOLLY
Stop it.

                         TURK
Why?

                         MOLLY
I don't know.

                         TURK
I don't mean to be so
forward. I'll walk on out of here
if you want. I just know that I've
never been around someone so
special before.

                         MOLLY
I'm not that special.

                    TURK
          To me you are. I've never felt
          this way around anyone else. I've
          never talked this much... I've
          never felt as good as I feel when I
          hear you sing. And to know that
          you've only sung for me... makes it
          even more special.

                    MOLLY
          I didn't sing for you.

Turk laughs.

                    TURK
          Okay, I can take a hint. It was
          wonderful listening to you. And
          talking. Take care.

                    MOLLY
          I... I can sing something for you
          if you want.

                    TURK
          Really?

                    MOLLY
          Sure.

                    TURK
          I'm honored.

                    MOLLY
          Anything in particular?

                    TURK
          Know any Duran Duran?

Molly laughs.

                    MOLLY
          No.

                    TURK
          You have a nice laugh too.

                    MOLLY
          Stop with the compliments!

                    TURK
          Fine. Sing me something and I
          promise to hate it.

                        MOLLY
          Hey!

                        TURK
          Just kidding... please sing. I'd
          love to hear anything you want to
          sing. And I'll try my best not to
          hit on you after.

                        MOLLY
          It's not that I don't like it... I
          mean... I don't... but it's okay...
          I mean... you know that we're in
          church and... well... and we just
          met... well, not really... but
          we...

                        TURK
          You're too cute.

                        MOLLY
          Stop!

                        TURK
          Okay... okay... I'm stopping.

                        MOLLY
          No more hitting on me.

                        TURK
          You mean today or forever.

Molly smiles shyly.

                        MOLLY
          Just today.

                        TURK
          It's a deal. Sing for me?

                        MOLLY
          I'll sing... but for God. I'll
          sing for you another day.

                        TURK
          Deal.

Molly sings "It Is Well With My Soul."

                        MOLLY
          "When peace like a river attendeth
          my way,
          When sorrows like sea billows roll,
                    (MORE)

                                        (CONTINUED)

                              MOLLY (cont'd)
          Whatever my lot, Thou hast taught
          me to say,
          'It is well, it is well with my
          soul.'

          Though Satan should buffet, though
          trials should come,
          Let this blest assurance control:
          That Christ hath regarded my
          helpless estate,
          And has shed His own blood for my
          soul.

          And Lord, haste the day when my
          faith shall be sight,
          The clouds be rolled back as a
          scroll,
          The trump shall resound and the
          Lord shall descend,
          Even so, it is well with my soul."

                         END OF SCENE

SCENE 5

                  MOLLY
         (Sings)
"The Lord's my Shepherd, I'll not
want. He makes me down to lie In
pastures green; He leadeth me The
quiet waters by. My soul He doth
restore again; And me to walk doth
make Within the paths of
righteousness, Even for His own
Name's sake. Yea, though I walk in
death's dark vale, Yet will I fear
none ill; For Thou art with me; and
Thy rod And staff me comfort still.
My table Thou hast furnished In
presence of my foes; My head Thou
dost with oil anoint, And my cup
overflows. Goodness and mercy all
my life Shall surely follow me; And
in God's house forevermore My
dwelling place shall be."

Lights come up on Molly and Turk. Turk is sleeping and
Molly is kneeling by him. Turk looks calm and no longer
hurting. Others are resting as well. Art is at the
door. Delia wakes and goes to him and takes over the watch.

                  ART
They're gone now.

                  DELIA
Get some rest.

                  ART
Thanks for keeping watch.

                  DELIA
Better safe than sorry and you need
some rest.

Art goes to Bea.

                  ART
How are you feeling?

                  BEA
Better... the energy here is so
different now... something has
happened.

(CONTINUED)

                    ART
Something good?

                    BEA
Yes... Molly is the key... the key
we've been looking for. She can
change this.

                    ART
How?

                    BEA
I don't know... but we have to find
out.

Art lays down on a pew to rest. Bea eats. Turk opens his
eyes and smiles at Molly.

                    TURK
You saved me, Molly.

                    MOLLY
I did.

                    TURK
How is that possible?

                    MOLLY
I don't know.

                    TURK
No one ever recovers from that. No
one ever comes back.

                    MOLLY
I'm so glad you did. I felt like a
part of me was missing when they
got you... like I wasn't complete
any more.

                    TURK
And I never could get too far from
you. Even when the creatures found
shelter in the darkness, I couldn't
stay away. Even though the sun
burned me like the fires of Hell, I
couldn't stay away from you. No
matter what evil they were
saying... no matter what messages
were in my head... somehow I
couldn't be apart from you. Our
souls are connected... they
couldn't break that bond.

They embrace.

>   MOLLY
>   I'm so happy to have you in my arms
>   again. I never want to let go.

Jude comes over. Turk looks annoyed.

>   JUDE
>   What kind of messages? What were
>   they saying?

Turk doesn't want to talk to Jude but Molly gives Turk an
encouraging nod.

>   TURK
>   They are hungry for death. And not
>   the kind of death we normally think
>   of but a walking death where they
>   rip the souls from us. But they
>   couldn't take mine... not without
>   Molly.

>   JUDE
>   You have a special bond that most
>   people don't have. They couldn't
>   break that.

>   TURK
>   That made them so angry. They
>   didn't think anything was that
>   strong. They wanted Molly so
>   badly. But not just because of the
>   bond... something more is inside
>   you, Molly. Something they
>   feared. A purity. A simple
>   purity, uncorrupted by the world.

>   MOLLY
>   Why would they fear that?

>   JUDE
>   Everyone has a little evil inside
>   them... perhaps you don't.

>   MOLLY
>   But I'm not perfect.

>   JUDE
>   But you're not evil either.

                              TURK
                You've never done anything bad.

                              MOLLY
                But I'm not as good as others...
                there are so many people at church
                who are so much better than I am.

                              JUDE
                They appear that way... but what do
                they do when we don't see them?

                              TURK
                You're good all the time.

                              MOLLY
                I'm really not.

                              TURK
                You never want to do anything bad.

                              MOLLY
                I don't. I do want to be good.

                              JUDE
                That's the most important thing...
                the desire to be good. If we think
                about that in all things we do,
                we'd all be going down the right
                path.

                              MOLLY
                I can't be the only one? And why
                would it matter?

                              TURK
                I did learn that we aren't the only
                ones who survived.

                              MOLLY
                There are others like us out there.

                              TURK
                Yes... so we're not alone.

                              JUDE
                Thank God in heaven for that.

                              MOLLY
                We have to get to them. We have to
                find them somehow.

                    JUDE
          Perhaps that is what we should
          do. Maybe that's our purpose.

Bea has joined them.

                    BEA
          Together we'll be stronger.

                    MOLLY
          How do we find them? Where do we
          go?

                    TURK
          Anywhere you see those creatures
          massing... that's where you'll find
          others like us.

                    BEA
          And we gather at a cathedral.

                    JUDE
          I hope we can fill it... fill it
          with hundreds of survivors.

                    TURK
          What do we do once we have them
          all?

                    MOLLY
          We sing. Sing until the evil is
          gone.

                    BEA
          Or until God hears us and brings us
          home.

Molly starts singing "He Leadeth Me" and the other join in
at the chorus:

                    MOLLY
          He leadeth me, O blessed thought! O
          words with heav'nly comfort
          fraught! Whate'er I do, where'er I
          be Still 'tis God's hand that
          leadeth me.

                    ALL
          He leadeth me, He leadeth me, By
          His own hand He leadeth me; His
          faithful foll'wer I would be, For
          by His hand He leadeth me.

                    (MORE)

                              ALL (cont'd)
                    Sometimes 'mid scenes of deepest
                    gloom, Sometimes where Eden's
                    bowers bloom, By waters still, o'er
                    troubled sea, Still 'tis His hand
                    that leadeth me.

                    Lord, I would place my hand in
                    Thine, Nor ever murmur nor repine;
                    Content, whatever lot I see, Since
                    'tis my God that leadeth me.

                    And when my task on earth is done,
                    When by Thy grace the vict'ry's
                    won, E'en death's cold wave I will
                    not flee, Since God through Jordan
                    leadeth me.

                         END OF SCENE

SCENE 6 - LIFE IS LIKE A BOX OF DIAPERS

Flashback to Art and Bea walking with a stroller.

>   ART
>   A baby is an amazing thing isn't
>   it?

>   BEA
>   A miracle.

>   ART
>   How does it happen? I mean I know
>   how it happens but... How? You
>   know what I mean?

Bea laughs...

>   BEA
>   I have no clue what you mean.

>   ART
>   It's so hard to do anything...
>   Finish my taxes, find the tv
>   remote... Cook something without
>   burning it...

>   BEA
>   Those are your challenges, yes.

>   ART
>   Funny...

>   BEA
>   I thought so.

>   ART
>   Anyway... I was making a point.

>   BEA
>   Go ahead.

>   ART
>   Even though we... I mean I can't do
>   those ordinary tasks... we can make
>   this beautiful work of art.

>   BEA
>   Hear that, Stinky... You're a work
>   of art.

Art laughs in surprise.

(CONTINUED)

                    ART
          Don't call her Stinky.

                    BEA
          But she is.

Art sniffs.

                    ART
          She is, isn't she?

                    BEA
          Still in awe and wonder at the
          little miracle?

                    ART
          I'm in awe at how much she can
          poop... How can such a little one
          make a big mess?

Bea looks in stroller.

                    BEA
          Don't worry... It's just gas.

                    ART
          That's a metaphor for life if I've
          ever heard one.

                    BEA
          What?

                    ART
          We think a big stink mean a major
          mess but sometimes there's no
          substance.

                    BEA
          A diaper is a metaphor for life?

                    ART
          It is if you think about it.

                    BEA
          I'd rather not.

                    ART
          You must hold all the disgusting
          things inside of you and if someone
          doesn't help you, then it leaks or
          bursts. But if there is a continued
          cleansing and renewal, then we live
          a more healthy and satisfied life.

                         BEA
          Like is like a box of diapers.

                         ART
          Something like that.

                         BEA
          I will never look at diaper
          changing the same way again.

                    END OF PLAY

ADAPTED MONOLOGUE 1 - HUNGRY FOR DEATH

                    TURK
They are hungry for death. And not
the kind of death we normally think
of but a walking death where they
rip our souls from us. But they
couldn't take mine... not without
you. You are my anchor, the anchor
that held me to this world... There
is a bond between us that protected
my soul.

That made them so angry. They
didn't think anything was that
strong. They wanted you so badly.
But not just because of the bond...
something more is inside you.
Something they feared. A purity. A
simple purity, uncorrupted by the
world.

I never could get too far from you.
Even when the creatures found
shelter in the darkness, I couldn't
stay away. Even though the sun
burned me like the fires of Hell, I
needed to be close to you. No
matter what evil they were
saying... no matter what messages
were in my head... somehow I
couldn't be apart from you. Our
souls are connected... they
couldn't break that bond.

I have to protect you now. They are
after you now. They want the power
inside you. I can hear them
chanting over and over again...

She is the one. She is the reason.
She is the beginning and the end.
Alpha and Omega. Yin and Yang. She
will bring balance.

                END OF MONOLOGUE

ADAPTED MONOLOGUE 2 - I WAS NEVER IMPORTANT

MOLLY

I wish I knew what that was all about... What does this all have to do with me? I never was important before. I never was special. I'm not the most religious person. I was in the church choir because I loved to sing. I didn't really do much else. I've lived a good enough life but nothing unique... nothing miraculous. I don't know what to do. I have no direction. How can I do something important when I don't even feel important. I didn't chose this mission... I didn't ask God to make me a vessel or some tool. I didn't chose this, God. I didn't ask for this.

I'm not strong enough. I'll fail.

But if there is some way to help Turk... If I have the power to do that. I want to save him.

He protected me... but he knew something was different... something was very wrong. We tried to keep away from others... we didn't want anyone else to get hurt. But he was injured... and I had to find help.

I have to do something... I can't stand by and let this happen to him... It was so horrible what happened to the others... I can't watch that happen to him too. I have to fight back.

END OF MONOLOGUE

ADAPTED MONOLOGUE 3 - FREE OF THE EVIL

                    ART
We all have in our own ways to
survive. That's why we're all still
free. Free of the evil that
consumed the others. Free of the
swarm.

We've spent so much time hiding in
churches and gathering supplies...
Always running... With the those
creatures always finding us...
Never being able to settle in one
place for long...

We just wanted to be in one place
long enough to feel normal again...
Alone in our own little world...
Turn the nightmare in to a dream,
find some calm in the storm, a
moment of peace... even for a short
time... But everywhere we went
went, it was always the same. They
would find us.

This is the first time something
different has happened. This is
new. We've never found so many
others like us... and never had so
many of them after us.

It's time to take a stand ... If
it's the end, may it be the end of
evil... The end of those creatures
... And the beginning of a new life
for us all.

                END OF MONOLOGUE

ADAPTED MONOLOGUE 4 - TRUST IN GOD?

                    DELIA
          I fear God. I don't trust him. I am
          afraid what he is going to do. I am
          afraid of what will happen every
          day... If I go outside, what will
          be waiting for me? There's
          something wrong out there.
          Something's not right.

          How can I trust trust in God? How
          can I trust the one who took my
          father away? How can I trust the
          one who turned my mother into a
          drunk? How I trust the one who put
          me in the house of someone who
          abused me? Every day I lived in
          fear. What would happen if I
          stepped outside my room? I didn't
          know what was waiting for me. I
          never knew what would wake up that
          day. The creep, the angry one, the
          monster... I didn't even want to
          get out of bed anymore. It got too
          hard. I was too scared. I would
          hide and pray to God to help me.
          But God never did. My childhood was
          gone and my only escape was
          adulthood.

          Even if God didn't do it why did he
          let it happen? I can't handle it...
          I'm going crazy.. The fear is
          crippling me... I have to drag
          myself out of bed and force myself
          to live each day... Sure, I put on
          this happy face... People think I
          am pretty cheerful... No one cares
          to see the pain under my skin...
          The pain that's ripping at my soul.

                    END OF MONOLOGUE

Printed in Great Britain
by Amazon.co.uk, Ltd.,
Marston Gate.